YAK! YAK! YAK! BLAH! BLAH! BLAH!

Cartoons by Henry Martin

Charles Scribner's Sons   *New York*

Acknowledgments

Selections in this collection have previously been published in various magazines. Selections are reprinted with the permission of *The Rotarian, Punch, Modern Maturity* and *NRTA* Journal, *Friends* Magazine, *Sign* Magazine. A selection is reprinted from the July 1974 issue of *Family Circle* Magazine, © 1974 The Family Circle Inc. Selections are from *The Christian Science Monitor,* © 1969, 1974, 1975, 1976 TCSPS. Selections are included by courtesy of *Better Homes & Gardens,* © Meredith Corporation 1974, 1975, 1976. All rights reserved. Of the 196 drawings in this book 23 first appeared in the *New Yorker,* copyright © 1967, 1968, 1969, 1970, 1971, 1972, 1973, 1974, 1975, 1976 The New Yorker Magazine, Inc.

Library of Congress Cataloging in Publication Data

Martin, Henry R
    Yak! Yak! Yak! Blah! Blah! Blah!

    Cartoons.
    1. Marriage—Caricatures and cartoons. 2. American wit and humor, Pictorial. I. Title.
NC1429.M4242A58   741.5'973   77-23939
ISBN 0-684-15126-X

1 3 5 7 9 11 13 15 17 19 V/C 20 18 16 14 12 10 8 6 4 2

Printed in the United States of America

FOR
019 - 24 - 9734
WITH ALL MY
LOVE
345 - 26 - 4155

"Oh, Lynn darling, if we could only freeze-dry this moment."

"He said it with candy. He said it with flowers. And now, he's said it with T-shirts!"

"*Agnes Guilton? This is Scott Warburton. I've selected your number at random from the telephone book. Fate has drawn us together but the rest is up to us. How about dinner Saturday night?*"

"Don't get me wrong, Rod. I _do_ like your life-style. It's _you_ I
don't like."

"Wow! I thought that I would never see a poem lovely as a tree, but <u>this</u>, Arthur, has markedly altered my original thinking."

"Say, how would you like to come home for dinner and meet the little Ms.?"

"Oh dear, I'm afraid I can't promise you anyone tall, dark, and handsome. Would you settle for healthy, wealthy, and wise?"

10

"I'll bet you thought I was going to be late to my own wedding, didn't you?"

"Do you, Jon, promise to love, honor, cherish, and help out a little around the house until death do you part?"

"Do you, Arthur, take thee, Alice, to have and to hold through tennis elbow, the green plague, bursitis, mono, bad backs, the golly wobbles, trick knee, muscle spasms, the midnight blues, pinched nerves, the heebie-jeebies, disk trouble, pulled tendons, the blue funk . . .?"

"The bride wore an antique Belgian lace shawl over a neon-green Nathan's Famous T-shirt."

"*Darling, you gave me the moon, the sun, and the stars—now I'd like a vacuum cleaner.*"

"Frank, my career; Frank, my career; Frank, my career . . ."

"Here she is, folks—that little rose-covered cottage you've always dreamed about. Forty-two five asking, $90 monthly in taxes, $50 monthly for utilities, $10 monthly for water, and 25¢ monthly in bone meal for the roses."

"Harold! Harold! Wake up! The clocks have stopped and the calendar's blank!"

"Monday morning! Well, shall I fire off the opening salvo in the continuing battle of the sexes for this week, fathead?"

"I want to take this opportunity to wish you and your symptoms, real and imaginary, a happy day."

"On your feet! It is the happy hour minus ten hours and count-
ing."

"And who have I the pleasure of breakfasting with this morning: Mr. Sleepyhead, Mr. Not-in-the-Mood-to-Talk, Mr. Grump, Mr. Lay Off, Alice, or Mr. Button Up, Alice?"

"Good morning, love! Today marks the seven thousand six hundred and sixty-fifth breakfast of our union, including upwards of 7,665 glasses of freshly squeezed orange juice, 15,130 slices of toast, 10,683 cups of coffee, and between 4,200 and 6,300 eggs up sunny-side. How do those statistics grab you?"

"I think spring is here, Alice. I've seen a robin, the forsythia is about to pop, and there was just a trace of a smile on Hersholt this morning."

"Forty-two degrees and cloudy with chance of showers ending in late afternoon. Dinner at eight tonight at the McDowells. Informal. Good-bye, dear, and have a nice day."

"On your way home tonight, pick up a loaf of pumpernickel, a dozen eggs, and a teensy spark of humanity, will you, Mervin?"

"*I'm going to buy my first wig today, Ewing, so be thinking of some wry little comment to make when you see me wearing it tonight.*"

"Here's a little reminder to pick up the dry cleaning and here's a little note to remind you to read the little reminder to pick up the dry cleaning."

"If it's not too late, Albert, set the world on fire!"

"Good luck at City Hall."

"I think I'll fix myself a cup of coffee. What's the correct time?"

"She'll have the Businessman's Lunch and I'll have the, uh, Ms.
Special."

"Can Howard Sr. come out and play?"

"It's your typical Tuesday mail: two occupants, three residents, one boxholder, and a rare opportunity to buy a ten-volume handsomely bound encyclopedia of world treasures."

"Well, if this is to be the winter of our discontent then I expect I'll need a new coat of some kind."

"Remember Helen Trent? Did she ever get Gill?"

"I'm terribly sorry, but what with the church rummage sale, the PTA white elephant sale, the Firemen's Flea Market, our own garage sale, the hospital auction, the children's lawn sale, the Rescue Mission, and the Salvation Army, we're pretty well cleaned out."

"Roses are red.
Violets are blue.
The landlord's here
And the rent is due."

"Well, today I begin my wonderfully perceptive and cogent book, abounding in brilliant insights—with ninety-six superb full-color illustrations. Fourteen-ninety-five to January. Twenty dollars thereafter."

"Have you told your readers about me? About how I walked into your life when all your friends and family had turned their backs on you? And about how I brought you love and hope for a brighter tomorrow?"

"Gunther, dear, I feel it is time to call upon the services of an architect to design a library to house your papers."

"Alice and I graduated from prep school in 1949, from Holyoke and Princeton in 1953, married in 1954, three children born in '55, '57, and '60. The older two are at Smith and Yale, the youngest, at Exeter. Alice has made the hospital volunteer team and Colonial Dames. I became president of my company in 1975. We feel we're on schedule."

"Now, have you got everything, Claude? Your boarding pass? Your flight bag? Your parachute? Your threatening note? Your pistol?"

"Harold, what's come over you?"

"Everything we own can be tumble-dried."

"Admit it, Fred. Utopia to you is the house at Pooh Corner, isn't it?"

50

"Honestly, Harry, you're a textbook example of a middle-aged man."

"I'm drawing up a list of all my good points and all my flaws, and so far my good points are running way, way ahead of my flaws."

"In your honor, Bertha, Otis is wearing his tea shirt."

"And Friday night the Bensons are here for dinner. Honestly, Albert, you don't remember <u>half</u> the data I feed you."

"I think the red flag signifies they've had a knock-down-drag-out fight and visitors are most unwelcome."

"The lights of the city have provided a twinkling backdrop. Your guests are gathered, and the curtain has risen on a light-hearted scene. It's time, my darling, for you to make your grand entrance."

"Besides macramé and needlepointing, Emily is into cooking, washing, dusting, vacuuming, and carpooling."

TONIGHT : 8 P.M.
FIRST NEIGHBORHOOD
SHOWING OF
JOHN & MARTHA'S
SLIDES OF THEIR
GREEK ISLANDS CRUISE

"Look, Taffy! Look! Look! There you are as a little puppy!"

"Harold! Have you been drinking?"

" 'Won't you come into my parlor?' said the flider to the spy."

"Happy days are here again!"

"Mrs. Preston is not at home at the moment. She's attending an annual store-wide sale with savings of up to thirty percent on all household items now through Friday. All sales are final. For details on how to get there see your paper."

"Lord, woman, where would the malls of America be without you?"

"O.K., Alice, spin the wheel and let's see who gets paid this week."

"Aren't you glad we grew up in a time when our parents could afford good schools, travel, medical care, gas and electricity, food, clothing, and shelter?"

"We're no longer living beyond our means. We're living beyond J. Paul Getty's means."

"I wish you'd forget about the city's fiscal troubles and come take a look at your own."

"I've consolidated all our debts into one low, easy-payment loan, and now I'm saying good-bye to all our worries."

"From now on you will take out the garbage every night without a whimper, give me a little cost of living raise, and always remember our anniversary without my reminding you."

"When you wake up, you will think you are Rhett Butler and I am Scarlett O'Hara."

"Give him the ability to take it as well as dish it out."

"Larry and I spent last night restructuring priorities in our major consumer purchases, and now my vacuum cleaner heads the list."

"Oh, just because I said he couldn't have the car next Saturday to go fishing. Now don't tell _me_ there isn't a male menopause!"

"Why don't you look where you're going, you stupid male chauvinist piglet!"

"Why, I'm delighted you asked, young lady! It stands for Male Chauvinist Pig Power."

"We want equal pay for women, free abortions, day-care centers, and Martha Washington, Martha Jefferson, Edith Roosevelt, and Mary Todd Lincoln carved on Mount Rushmore."

"I have something to tell you, Alfred. Promise you won't get mad. Alice Logan and I joined a women's lib group."

"It has been moved and seconded that we turn everything over to women and go fishing."

"It is I, Franklin, the father figure, home to the family unit and ready for interaction."

"Guess what? On the way home I passed GO and collected two hundred dollars."

"I don't have a hat to keep off the rain because I ate my hat when I lost a bet that I'd eat my hat if we should have rain today."

"Look, Arnie! Isn't this sweet? While we were out it paid the bills, balanced the checkbooks, addressed the Christmas cards, and planned the meals for 1977."

"This is perfectly ridiculous. I want you both to turn around and look at each other and say you're sorry."

"Dear diary: Harold to station 7:15, carpool 7:45, cleaning woman 8:15, Jessie to dentist 10:15, hairdresser 10:30, Jessie from dentist 11:15, grocery 11:30, luncheon 12:30, carpool 2:30, Jessie piano 2:45, Tim hockey 3, Ted band 3, Jessie lacrosse 4, Ted braces 4:10, cleaning woman bus 4:15, kids home 5:15, cat to vet 5:30, Harold station 6:30, dinner 6:30, Jessie interact 7:15, Tim scouts 7:30, Ted basketball 7:30, Harold township meeting 8, me adult school 8 . . ."

"In his youth, Joe was a defender of faith, a seeker of truth, and a protector of beauty. Now he's a drinker of beer and a watcher of TV."

"Dr. and Mrs. T. Arlington Hunsucker request the pleasure of our company at the Tupperware party in honor of their daughter on Saturday, the 28th . . ."

"I don't care, Arthur, <u>how</u> rarely we see the Jepsons, we're sending them an invitation to Beebee's wedding. After all, they nicked us for a present last June when fat Florence plopped down the aisle in her hand-me-down Belgian lace."

"Could I have her call you back? The washing machine has flooded, the canary has escaped, there's a salesman at the door, Freddie just threw up, and she's about to lose her cool."

"Hi, there! We're macaws, genus <u>Ara</u>, common in South and Central America. We are called macaws because we feed on the fruit of macaw palms. We are gregarious but monogamous. If you have a moment, I'd like you to meet the little woman."

"Oh, and there's Mommy and Daddy in 1968 just after we met in a campus disturbance."

". . . and so the Prince married the Princess and they lived happily until the outbreak of the revolution."

"Mary had a little lamb . . . at $1.75 a pound."

"Now that Jon Jr., Alice, little Nan, Frankie, Judy, and Jill are in school, Jon, I'm going to look for a job. We could use the extra income for education."

"Mommy and Daddy are not mad at <u>you</u>, Marilyn. Mommy and Daddy are mad at the naughty thing you've done."

"Would you mind turning down the volume, Son? Your mother and I are trying to get on with our lives of quiet desperation."

"This is your dad, Son. Your mother and I think it's time you stopped collecting degrees and came home."

"Well, Doris, the children are grown and gone, and now it's just you versus me."

"Hi! I'm Gretchen Comstock, your wife of thirty years. Now that the children are grown and gone I thought we ought to get reacquainted."

"Don't 'shush, the children will hear' me, Alice. The children are grown and gone and your 'shush, the children will hear' days are over."

"I love you,
Artie."

"Yeah? And just what's
that supposed to mean?"

"How do I love thee? Let me count the way—singular."

"In the future, when I give you a 'come hither' look, you come hither on the double."

"Where's your lord and master?"

"If I'm not the man you married, Agnes, why gracious goodness, who do you suppose I am and how come I'm living here?"

"You said no such thing, Emily! Just for the record, let me play back that conversation of February 23, 1967."

"First of all, a Leo has no business whatsoever marrying a Virgo."

"Ga-a-a-a-h ha-a-a-a-h! Choing!"

"Children, your father won't be home for dinner. I poked a little good-natured fun at him. He couldn't take it and ran home to Grandma's apron strings."

"Happy Valentine, sweetie-pie!"

"All of a sudden I noticed she was saying _my_ daughter, _my_ son, _my_ silver, _my_ furniture, _my_ house, and _your_ friends, _your_ troubles, _your_ worries, _your_ problems, and _your_ fault."

"My analyst says that your analyst is as nutty as a fruitcake."

"It's the old story: Their first child was a love child, their second child was an attempt to hold the marriage together, their third was a rush of reconciliation, and their last was the sweet sorrow of parting."

"That's your solution to everything, isn't it, Orville?"

TO OUR
FRIENDS AND NEIGHBORS
—
ALICE IS IN RENO.
THE CHILDREN ARE
WITH ALICE'S FOLKS.
ALICE WILL GET THIS
HOUSE, CUSTODY OF THE
CHILDREN AND $1,000
MONTHLY SUPPORT.
—
YES, JUDY B. WAS
NAMED
CORESPONDENT.
FOR ADDITIONAL
INFORMATION
CALL
244- 9140
EVENINGS

"Our story began 'Once upon a time' and ended 'Divorce granted.'"

"Listen to this, residents of the State of New York! Alfred T. Gellermeyer is two months behind in his alimony payments!"

"This is my bride and these are my spin-offs from a previous sit-com."

"I don't want to play house anymore and I want custody of the dolls."

"Mr. O'Conner, your ignored mother, estranged wife, neglected children, and slighted friends are here to give you the raspberries."

"Fly over to him and see if the storm is over. If it is, bring back a sign of peace."

"I suppose we have Helen Gurley Brown to thank for this."

"Archie's definition of a good movie is one that has a beginning, a middle, and no end of sex."

"I'll bet if George M. Cohan were alive today he wouldn't be telling all the gang at Forty-second Street he'd soon be there."

" 'Mr. and Mrs. Sheldon Carter Sloane request the pleasure of your company at the reception of their daughter, Harriet, and Mr. Edward Arlo Sander in announcement of their living together . . .' "

"Remember 'Snug Harbor,' 'Bide-a-Wee,' and 'Dew Drop Inn'?"

"Edgar, are you fantasizing again?"

"Have you noticed, Myrna, that I'm getting more and more neurotic?"

"If you ask me, Enid, you've been seeing too many movies."

"Marvin may not hear you. He's into transcendental meditation, vitamins, acupuncture, primal therapy, Zen, natural foods, analysis, hypnosis, and yoga in one last desperate attempt to zap his migraines."

"I've reached that age when a good day is one when you get up and nothing hurts."

"Turn up your hearing aid, Otis. I didn't say Marjorie Thompson was in a bordello. I said she was into bargello."

"Do you have one that says, 'Good luck on your annual checkup'?"

"What's it say, Margaret? I'm still not used to these bifocals."

"With my new specs, Alice, everything has come into focus but you."

"Harvey has been rather depressed since his birthday. Some-
body gave him a shawl."

"This is Mrs. Garvin. Mr. Garvin won't be in today. Mr. Garvin is all pooped out."

"Now that you've lost your job I suppose you'll have more time to wear your leisure suits."

"As far back as 1937, Charles was saying, 'To hell with every-thing.' "

"I just totaled the Chrysler so <u>now</u> you have a care in the world."

"If you were to distill me, Zella, what would be the import of that distillation?"

"For thirty years, Alice, we have <u>not</u> done those things we ought not to have done and not left <u>un</u>done the things we ought to have done and there is no fun in us."

"Come on in, Mother. George and I are just having a little fun with ordinary things found around the average home."

"When Alex assumes that stance I never know if he's exploring life's mysteries, dreaming the impossible dream, pondering the universals, or just trying to create an impression."

"Wallace is refusing all media input save the Harvard Classics."

"Have you noticed, Edie, how the yesterdays are piling up and the tomorrows are dwindling?"

"Seasons Greetings to all our friends far and near! So much has happened to us this year I hardly know where to begin but since I'm no women's libber, I'll start with the head of the family, big Ed. Ed lost his job early in May and has been underfoot here and hitting the bottle when he should be out looking for a job. Little Ed who we thought held great promise as a surgeon was tossed out of med school on a possession-of-marijuana charge. Daphine, our high school sophomore, got herself pregnant and had an abortion. Little Fred . . ."

"Hold it, Hubert! It's Christmas Day in the morning and all stock exchanges, banks, and places of business are closed for the day!"

"If you're not doing anything after supper, Bayard, could you bring the Middle East into sharper focus for me?"

" 'Attended to the cats'?"   "Done!"
'Set table for breakfast'?"   "Done!"
'Locked up house'?"   "Done!"
'Turned off the lights'?"   "Done!"
'Turned down the heat'?"   "Done!"
'Turned on the night light'?"   "Done!"
'Set clock radio wake-up alarm'?" "Done!"

"I'll promise not to interrupt you with interesting quotes if you'll promise not to intrude on me with fascinating excerpts."

"Good night to you and your bursitis, your neuritis, your arthritis, your cystitis, your bronchitis, your angitis, your colitis, and last, but not least, your lousy lumbago."

"Before we sign off do you have a quick wrap-up, final word, or closing thought?"

"... and make that lump on the other side of the bed a little more supportive."

"Dear God, give Mr. Perfect a tiny flaw."

"For our anniversary this year, I'm preparing a one-man intimate revue highlighting the thirty-two years of our marriage."

"Today is Grandmother's birthday. If she were alive, she'd be one hundred and ten years young and rarin' to go."

"Year before last Albert thought his days were numbered. Last year he thought his time had come. This year he fears he'll reach the end of the line."

"Bertie, what do you say we get off our duffs and get this country going again?"

"If you don't mind, Innes, I don't think I'm up to your old tricks
tonight."

"Hi ya, hubby! Good 8,395th morning of our wedded bliss to you!"

"My day? Well, for openers, I tendered my resignation, converted all our holdings to cash, and signed up for a two-year hitch in the Peace Corps."

"I think I need a week or two at the shore to relax, take stock of myself, and see where I go from here."

"When Arthur hit fifty he jumped in the pool with all his clothes on."

"Say, Margaret, how about a skinny dip?"

"When retirement comes for Jesse next year, I'm harnessing his vast managerial expertise and thrusting him into a broader arena so he won't be underfoot."

"Happy birthday, Vic! My, my—sixty-five! I guess this marks the first day of the rest of our life savings!"

"Well, let's see, Margaret. Puttering, hanging around, loafing, getting underfoot, and goofing off are what I have on the docket for today."

"Could I have him call you back? This is his first day of retirement and he's busy downstairs frittering."

"These, Emily, are my retirement plans."

"It's your retirement anniversary, silly. Today marks a year you've been underfoot."

"To our next millennium together."

"Gee, for our fiftieth wouldn't you think there'd be more icing?"

"You're eighty-eight, Junius. Don't you think you'd better start reading the classics?"

"Whatever happened to names like Sunset Village, Golden Retreat, and Leisure Living?"

"Together, Norman and I represent 146 years of good clean living."

"I guess you realize that if I had married Waldo Fitzgibbons instead of you I'd be coasting down Memory Lane in a Bentley or a Rolls with a hell of a lot of beautiful memories of candlelight and wine and castles on the Rhine."

"Maybe we could hold our marriage together if we adopted a grandchild."

"Tell me, Ernest, would you like the Twenty-third Psalm to be read at your funeral?"

"On your left now is the grave of Elias Goodberry, founder of the Goodberry Grain & Feed Company, who set tongues wagging back in 1836 when he promenaded on the village green with the notorious Mae Belle Kelly."

"This was snapped of Roswell just before he took arms against a sea of troubles."

"Times and customs have changed, Charles. Take these plastic flowers . . ."

"You wish now you'd paid more attention to me when I attempted to explain to you about insurance and stocks and income tax, don't you?"

"As a touching gesture for our many well-wishers, could we pause a brief moment by my late husband's grave?"

1   Previously unpublished
2   *Look*, May 19, 1970
3   Previously unpublished
4   Previously unpublished
5   Previously unpublished
6   Previously unpublished
7   *Cosmopolitan*, April 1970
8   *Ladies' Home Journal*, September 1975
9   *Friends*, May 1976
10 *The New Yorker*, January 13, 1973
11 *Ladies' Home Journal*, June 1973
12 *Ladies' Home Journal*, December 1973
13 Previously unpublished
14 *The New Yorker*, March 29, 1976
15 Previously unpublished
16 *Good Housekeeping*, January 1971
17 *Ladies' Home Journal*, June 1974
18 *Ladies' Home Journal*, January 1973
19 *Christian Science Monitor*, January 23, 1975
20 *Ladies' Home Journal*, January 1973
21 Previously unpublished
22 Previously unpublished
23 Previously unpublished
24 Previously unpublished
25 Previously unpublished
26 Previously unpublished
27 *Christian Science Monitor*, May 13, 1974
28 *Christian Science Monitor*, March 17, 1969
29 *The Rotarian*, April 1973
30 Previously unpublished
31 Previously unpublished
32 *Christian Science Monitor*, March 3, 1970
33 *Washingtonian*, February 1971
34 *McCalls*, July 1970
35 Previously unpublished

36 *Christian Science Monitor*, October 26, 1976
37 *Christian Science Monitor*, March 15, 1975
38 *Christian Science Monitor*, August 3, 1976
39 *Christian Science Monitor*, December 10, 1975
40 Previously unpublished
41 *Better Homes & Gardens*, November 1974
42 Previously unpublished
43 *The New Yorker*, August 2, 1969
44 *The New Yorker*, June 26, 1971
45 *New York Times Book Review*, May 6, 1973
46 Previously unpublished
47 *The New Yorker*, November 25, 1972
48 *Modern Maturity*, February/March 1975
49 *NRTA Journal*, September/October 1976
50 *New York Times Book Review*, October 31, 1971
51 *Practical Psychology*, July 1975
52 *Better Homes & Gardens*, October 1975
53 Previously unpublished
54 *McCalls*, May 1968
55 Previously unpublished
56 *The Rotarian*, August 1976
57 Previously unpublished
58 Previously unpublished
59 *Modern Maturity*, April/May 1974
60 *Ladies' Home Journal*, October 1972
61 *The New Yorker*, March 17, 1975
62 *Ladies' Home Journal*, January 1972
63 *The New Yorker*, November 7, 1970
64 Previously unpublished
65 Previously unpublished
66 Previously unpublished
67 *Ladies' Home Journal*, February 1976
68 Previously unpublished
69 *Ladies' Home Journal*, February 1972
70 Previously unpublished
71 *The New Yorker*, December 13, 1969
72 *Modern Maturity*, October/November 1976
73 *Modern Maturity*, August/September 1975
74 *The Rotarian*, July 1972
75 *Consumer Report*, September 1970
76 *Cosmopolitan*, December 1973

77   *Ladies' Home Journal*, February 1972
78   *Modern Maturity*, October/November 1976
79   *Ladies' Home Journal*, June 1971
80   *Modern Maturity*, October/November 1976
81   *Modern Maturity*, October/November 1976
82   *The New Yorker*, June 6, 1970
83   *Punch*, October 6, 1976
84   *Ladies' Home Journal*, July 1970
85   *Friends*, March 1, 1976
86   Previously unpublished
87   *Ladies' Home Journal*, September 1973
88   Previously unpublished
89   Previously unpublished
90   *Better Homes & Gardens*, August 1976
91   *Friends*, September 1976
92   Previously unpublished
93   *Campus Life*, April 1976
94   *The Rotarian*, March 1975
95   Previously unpublished
96   Previously unpublished
97   *Ladies' Home Journal*, March 1974
98   *Phi Delta Kappan*, April 1976
99   *Ladies' Home Journal*, May 1972
100 *The Rotarian*, September 1975
101 *The New Yorker*, March 11, 1967
102 *The New Yorker*, October 11, 1969
103 Previously unpublished
104 Previously unpublished
105 *Sign*, February 1976
106 *New York Times Book Review*, January 31, 1971
107 Previously unpublished
108 Previously unpublished
109 Previously unpublished
110 *NRTA Journal*, May/June 1976
111 *The New Yorker*, June 15, 1974
112 *Good Housekeeping*, April 1969
113 Previously unpublished
114 Previously unpublished
115 Previously unpublished
116 Previously unpublished
117 Previously unpublished

118   Previously unpublished
119   Previously unpublished
120   *Sign*, July/August 1976
121   *Practical Psychology*, March 1976
122   *Phi Delta Kappan*, December 1969
123   *The New Yorker*, April 29, 1972
124   Previously unpublished
125   *The New Yorker*, July 8, 1967
126   Previously unpublished
127   Previously unpublished
128   Previously unpublished
129   *Ladies' Home Journal*, August 1970
130   *The New Yorker*, August 2, 1976
131   *The New Yorker*, May 11, 1968
132   *Medical Tribune*, September 17, 1975
133   *The New Yorker*, February 19, 1972
134   Previously unpublished
135   *New York Times*, February 16, 1975
136   Previously unpublished
137   Previously unpublished
138   *Washingtonian*, March 1973
139   *Washingtonian*, December 1970
140   *Family Circle*, July 1974
141   *American Legion*, March 1973
142   Previously unpublished
143   *Good Housekeeping*, September 1971
144   *The New Yorker*, September 30, 1967
145   *The Rotarian*, August 1973
146   *Practical Psychology*, April 1975
147   Previously unpublished
148   Previously unpublished
149   Previously unpublished
150   Previously unpublished
151   Previously unpublished
152   Previously unpublished
153   Previously unpublished
154   Previously unpublished
155   Previously unpublished
156   Previously unpublished
157   Previously unpublished
158   Previously unpublished

159   Previously unpublished
160   Previously unpublished
161   Previously unpublished
162   Previously unpublished
163   Previously unpublished
164   Previously unpublished
165   *Ladies' Home Journal*, March 1972
166   *The New Yorker*, November 25, 1974
167   *NRTA Journal*, May/June 1976
168   *The New Yorker*, February 14, 1970
169   Previously unpublished
170   *Sign*, October 1974
171   Previously unpublished
172   Previously unpublished
173   *Look*, June 24, 1969
174   Previously unpublished
175   *Harpers*, June 1969
176   *Look*, March 7, 1967
177   *Practical Psychology*, February 1976
178   Previously unpublished
179   Previously unpublished
180   Previously unpublished
181   Previously unpublished
182   *Better Homes & Gardens*, October 1974
183   Previously unpublished
184   *The New Yorker*, October 5, 1968
185   *Harpers*, March 1969
186   *The Rotarian*, March 1975
187   *The Rotarian*, September 1972
188   *New York Times*, January 25, 1976
189   Previously unpublished
190   *The New Yorker*, April 7, 1975
191   *The New Yorker*, September 5, 1970
192   Previously unpublished
193   *Washingtonian*, August 1969
194   Previously unpublished
195   Previously unpublished
196   Previously unpublished